The A-String Book for Viola

by Cassia Harvey

©2018 by C. Harvey Publications All Rights Reserved.

www.charveypublications.com

The A-String Book for Viola

Cassia Harvey

Long Bows on the A string

Playing the A string with "Mississippi Hot Dog"

©2018 C. Harvey Publications All Rights Reserved.

Writing the Note "A"

Copy the first measure here:

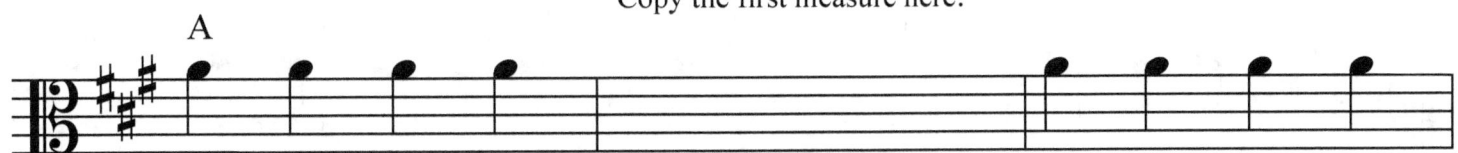

Write four "A" quarter notes.

Write four "A" quarter notes.

Rhythm Review

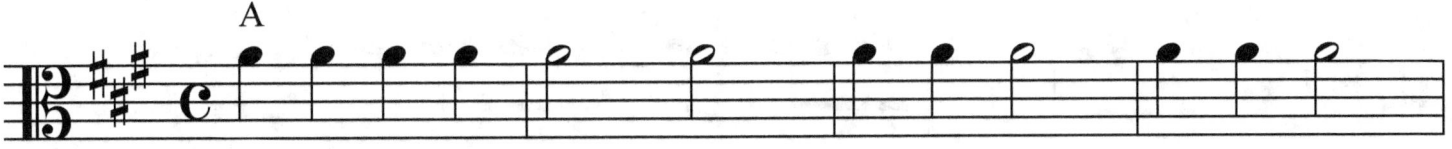

First Finger "B" on the A String

Rhythms with A and B

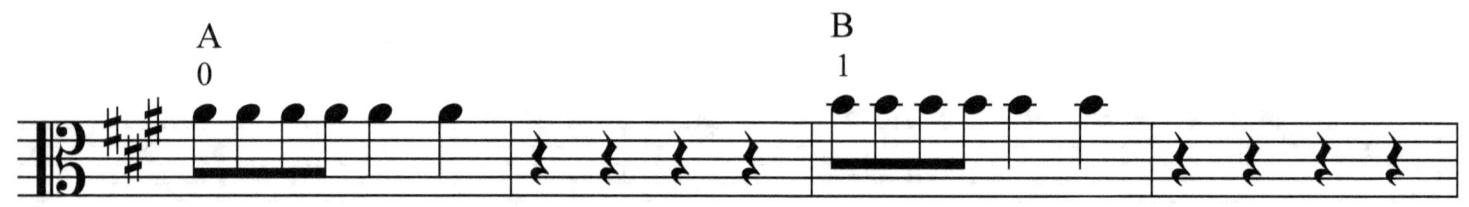

The A-String Book for Viola

A Peaceful March

Reviewing the Note "B"

©2018 C. Harvey Publications All Rights Reserved.

Learning Second Finger "C#"

Merrily We Roll Along

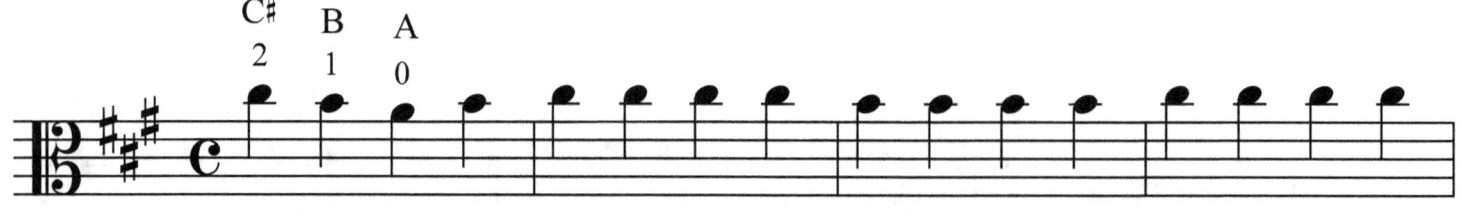

Hot Cross Buns with Variations

Go Tell Aunt Rhody

American Folk Tune

©2018 C. Harvey Publications All Rights Reserved.

Note-Name Study #1

A B C♯ B

A B A B

B C♯ B C♯

B C♯ B A

Note-Name Study #2

C♯ B A B

C♯ A C♯ B

A C♯ B C♯

A C♯ B A

Changing Notes More Quickly

In the Garden

Russian Folk Song

Alouette

French Folk Song

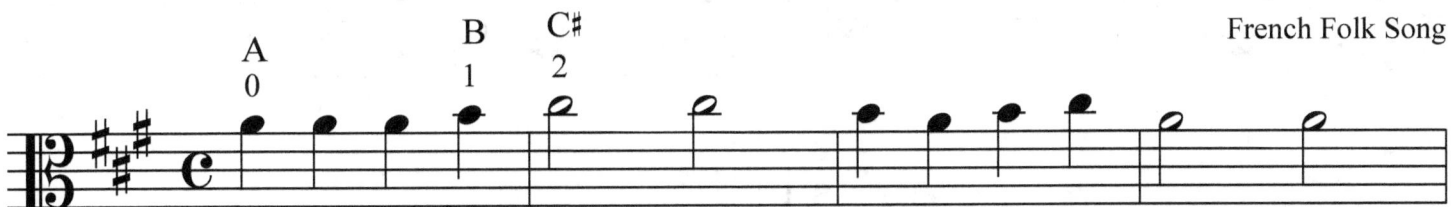

©2018 C. Harvey Publications All Rights Reserved.

Finger Trainer

Worms in the Garden

©2018 C. Harvey Publications All Rights Reserved.

Skipping to Second Finger

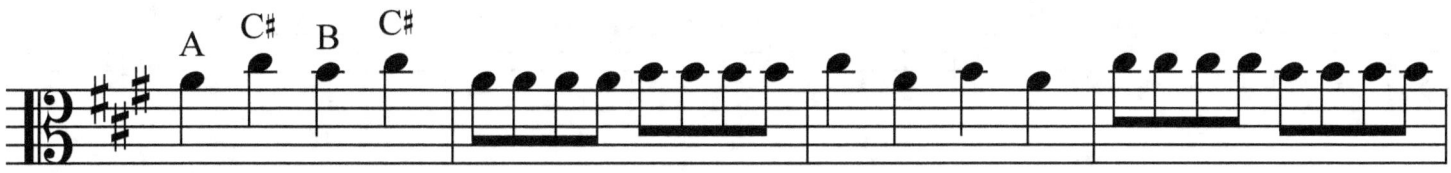

The Ladybug

Hungarian Folk Song

©2018 C. Harvey Publications All Rights Reserved.

Picking Vegetables

Little Dance

©2018 C. Harvey Publications All Rights Reserved.

Learning 3rd Finger "D"

Rhythm With the New Note "D"

Ragotin

French Folk Song

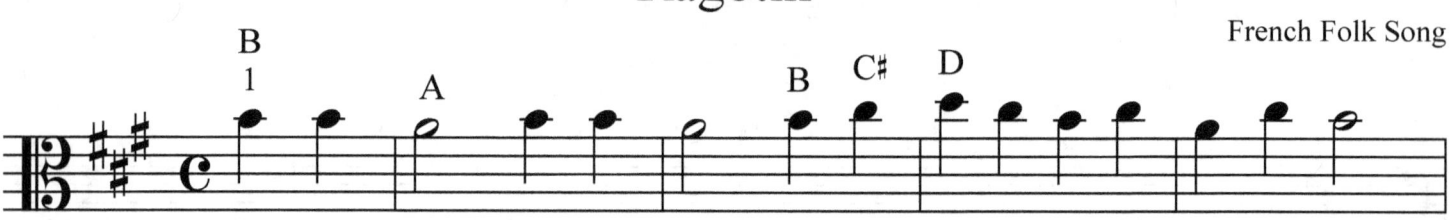

The Skipping Study

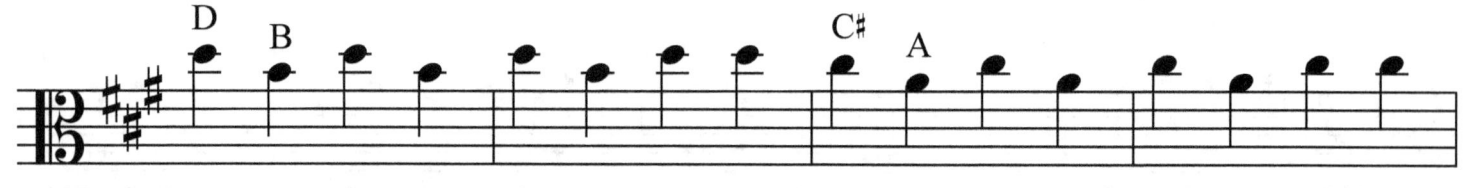

©2018 C. Harvey Publications All Rights Reserved.

The Scale Workout

Croatian Folk Song

On the Neva River

Russian Folk Song

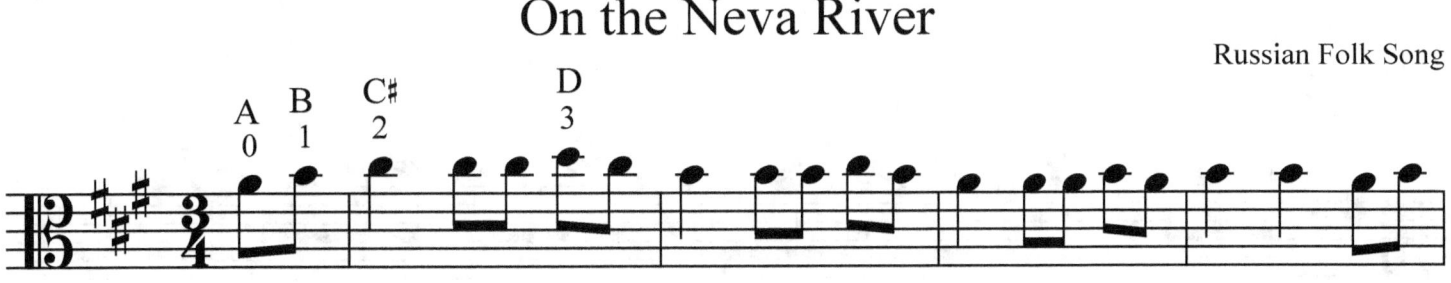

By Our Gates

Russian Folk Song

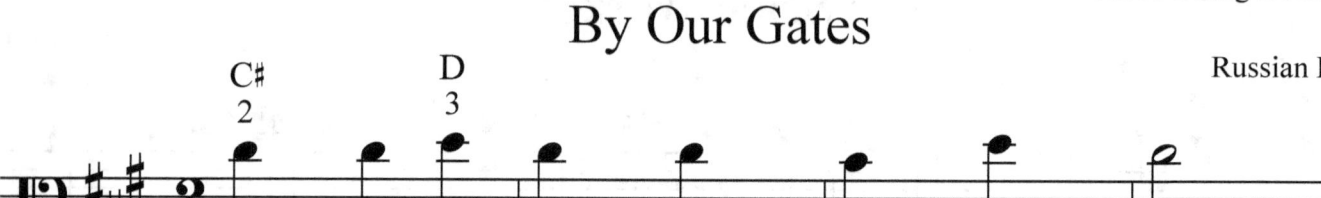
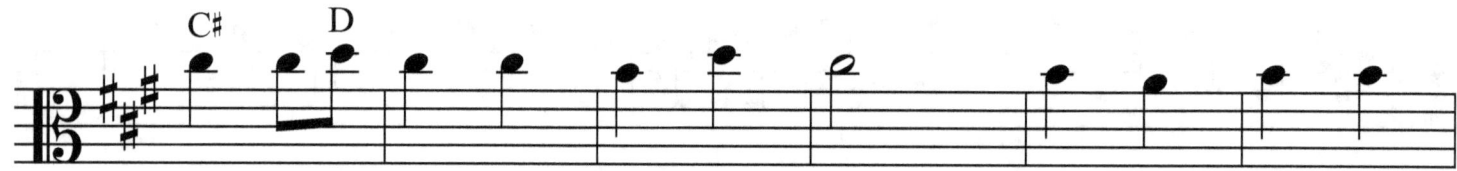

Exercise with "D"

©2018 C. Harvey Publications All Rights Reserved.

The A-String Book for Viola

March of the Sunflowers

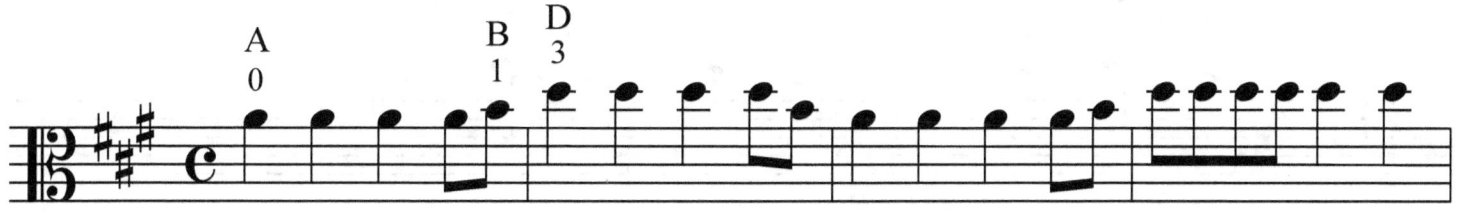

Counting Exercise

©2018 C. Harvey Publications All Rights Reserved.

Sad Memories

Running

Heroic March

Fiddle Tune

Learning 4th Finger "E"

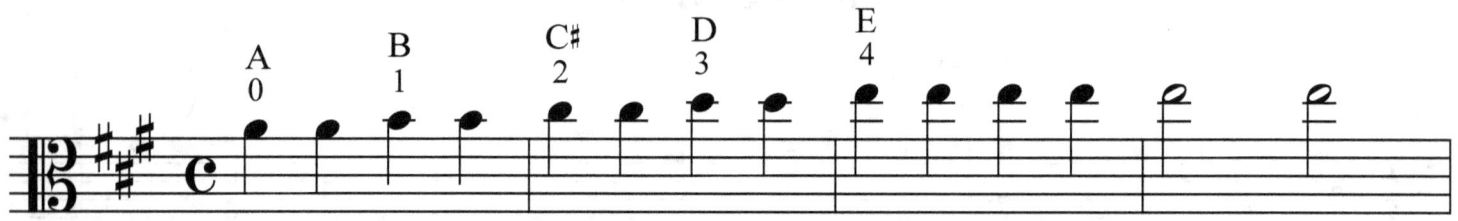

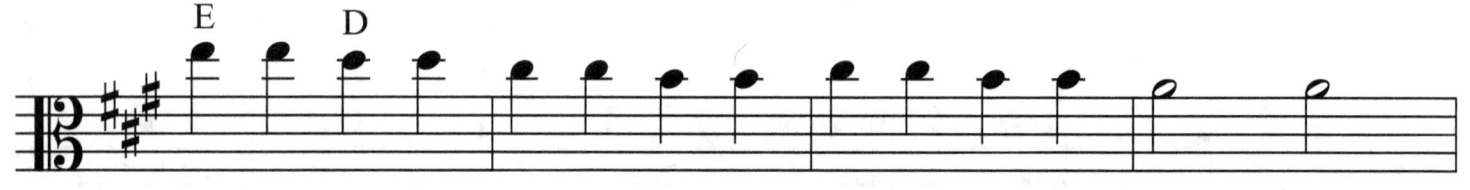

Drink to Me Only With Thine Eyes

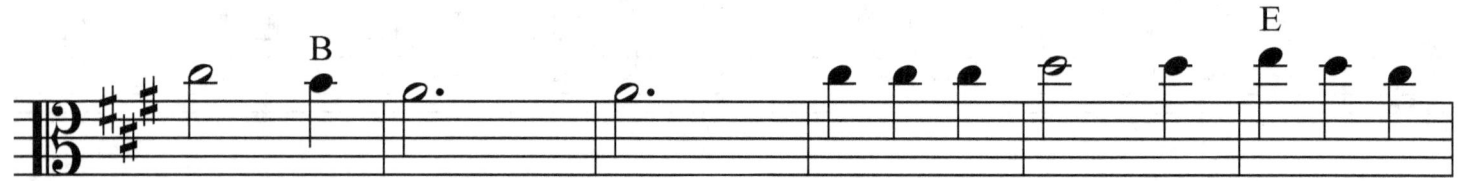

Using "E"

German Folk Dance

Big Skips

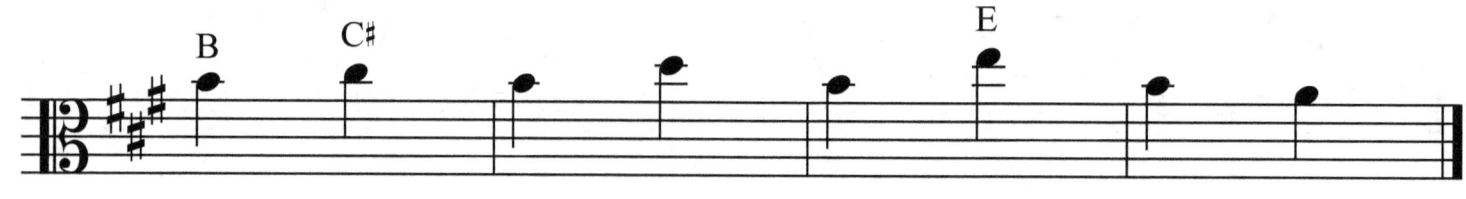

The Little Sheep

French Folk Song

An Awkward Exercise

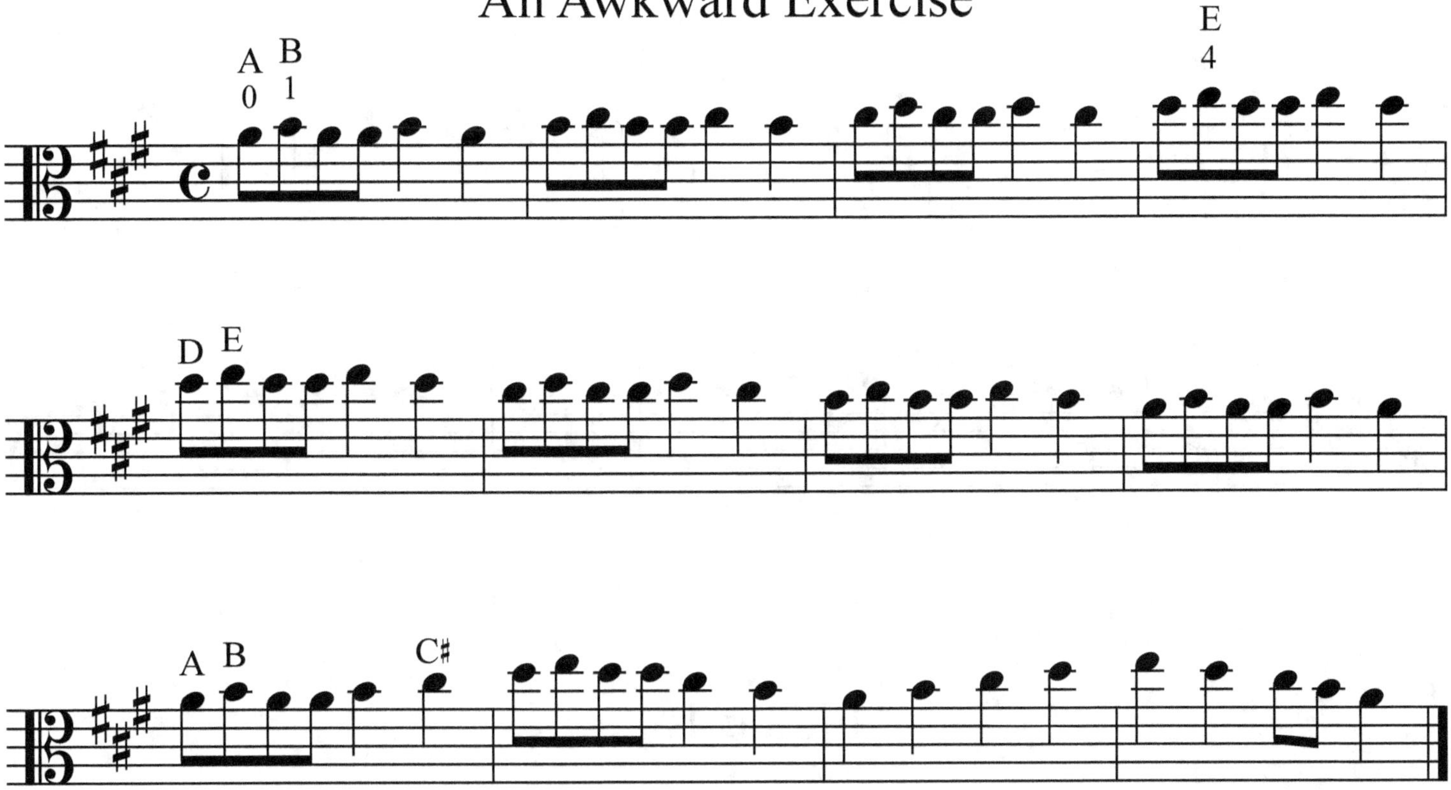

The Young Maid

Russian Folk Song

Walking and Skipping

Fiddle Tune

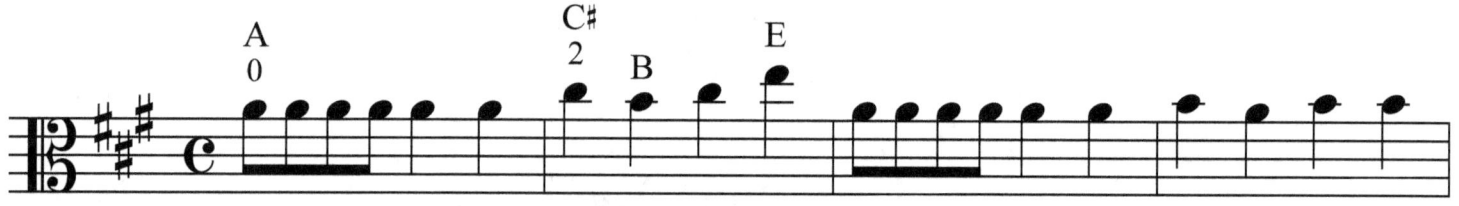

The A-String Book for Viola

Finger Twister

Don't Disturb the Wild Winds

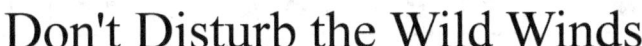

Russian Folk Song

©2018 C. Harvey Publications All Rights Reserved.

Warm-Up #1

Planting Grass by the River Bank

Russian Folk Song

©2018 C. Harvey Publications All Rights Reserved.

The A-String Book for Viola 27

Warm-Up #2

The Garden Blooms

Russian Folk Song

©2018 C. Harvey Publications All Rights Reserved.

available from www.charveypublications.com
Viola, Cello, and *Bass Book One*

Beginning Low-String Series:

These books combine fun songs and easy exercises to help beginning students play as much as possible. Teachers can use this book as a method for string classes at the beginning of their second year or as a supplemental study book for students who know a few notes but need more work on note-reading. These books can be played in private lessons, same-string classes, or in mixed-string classes.

Viola Book One   CHP295
Cello Book One   CHP221
Bass Book One   CHP245
***Viola, Cello, and Bass Book One* Score and Piano Accompaniment**   CHP306

www.ingramcontent.com/pod-product-compliance
Lightning Source LLC
Chambersburg PA
CBHW051431070526
44584CB00023B/3676